365

REASONS WHY GETTIN' OLD AIN'T SO BAD

KAREN O'CONNOR

HARVEST HOUSE PUBLISHERS

EUGENE, OREGON

Cover design by Dugan Design Group, Bloomington, Minnesota

Cover photo © iStockphoto / josteina

Published in association with the Books & Such Literary Agency, 52 Mission Circle, Suite 122, PMB 170, Santa Rosa, CA 95409-5370, www.booksandsuch.biz.

365 REASONS WHY GETTIN' OLD AIN'T SO BAD
Copyright © 2010 by Karen O'Connor
Published by Harvest House Publishers
Eugene, Oregon 97402
www.harvesthousepublishers.com

ISBN 978-0-7369-2859-5

Printed in the United States of America

10 11 12 13 14 15 16 17 18 / BP-SK / 10 9 8 7 6 5 4 3 2 1

Counting
Our Blessings

Several years ago I wrote *Gettin' Old Ain't for Wimps* (more than 250,000 copies sold), the first book of what became a bestselling series. It was great fun to collect experiences from people over 50 and turn them into humorous short stories that brought a chuckle, a smile, and, I hope, some inspiration to people of all ages.

Since then I've been enjoying my own adventure of getting older. It has its challenges, but there are many blessings too—among them are spoiling my grandchildren, receiving senior discounts, and being able to take a nap whenever I want to. So I decided to put together 365 reasons why getting old ain't so bad. I hope you'll enjoy them...even if you have a few years to go before admitting you're part of the older set.

Karen O'Connor

Gettin' old ain't so bad because...
you don't have to worry about
impressing anyone.

Gettin' old ain't so bad because...
you can enjoy a lifetime of memories
without having to relive them.

Gettin' old ain't so bad because...
you can take as many naps as you wish.

Gettin' old ain't so bad because...
you can watch the world change
without it raising your blood pressure.

Gettin' old ain't so bad because...
you can sleep in anytime you want to.

Gettin' old ain't so bad because...
at last you're wise and caring and have
time to show both.

Gettin' old ain't so bad because...
you finally notice and appreciate the "little things" in life.

Gettin' old ain't so bad because...
you and your mate, or you and your friends, are as comfy with one another as old sneakers.

Gettin' old ain't so bad because...
you can finally get out of debt and stay that way.

Gettin' old ain't so bad because...
you're probably a grandparent, maybe even a great-grandparent. What fun!

Gettin' old ain't so bad because...
staying home with your spouse is the best kind of date.

Gettin' old ain't so bad because...
heaven seems closer than ever.

Gettin' old ain't so bad because...
you can now be "friends" with your
adult children.

Gettin' old ain't so bad because...
you can take up hiking and golf and
knitting and fishing and writing and
skydiving and...

Gettin' old ain't so bad because...
you can sip tea with a friend without having to get back to work or home at a certain time.

Gettin' old ain't so bad because...
you can now volunteer your time and talents.

Gettin' old ain't so bad because...
you can relax and mind your own
business...for a change.

Gettin' old ain't so bad because...
you have time to think your own
thoughts without getting interrupted.

Gettin' old ain't so bad because...
you can take a short walk or a long
one...and stop as often as you wish.

Gettin' old ain't so bad because...
you can spend time listening to the birds, even learning their calls if you want to.

Gettin' old ain't so bad because...
you can learn to swim—even if you've never done it before.

Gettin' old ain't so bad because...
you now have time to travel—even if it's just to the next town and back.

Gettin' old ain't so bad because...
there are many new, fascinating people to meet.

Gettin' old ain't so bad because...
you can get a senior discount on almost anything. Don't forget to ask!

Gettin' old ain't so bad because...
you can get a tee time when younger golfers are at work.

Gettin' old ain't so bad because...
you can take advantage of the Early Bird Specials at your favorite eatery.

Gettin' old ain't so bad because...
if you need help you can ask for it
without apology.

Gettin' old ain't so bad because...
you can finally forgive yourself for
foolish mistakes and make a fresh start.

Gettin' old ain't so bad because...
you have time to watch the sunrise and
sunset without rushing to or from work.

Gettin' old ain't so bad because...
you have time to try your hand at
painting or sketching.

Gettin' old ain't so bad because...
you have more time for friends, and
they have more time for you.

Gettin' old ain't so bad because...
you can look in the mirror and honestly
say, "Not bad for an old geezer!"

Gettin' old ain't so bad because...
you can toss the hair dye and let your
gray locks shine.

Gettin' old ain't so bad because...
you can play Bingo or Bridge—and it
doesn't matter if you win or lose.

Gettin' old ain't so bad because...
your few extra pounds are good
padding if you fall.

Gettin' old ain't so bad because...
you can speak your mind without
defending yourself.

Gettin' old ain't so bad because...
you can make decisions for yourself—
regardless of what others think.

Gettin' old ain't so bad because...
it's fun to be told how young you
look—for your age.

Gettin' old ain't so bad because...
you can celebrate your birthday and be
proud of it.

Gettin' old ain't so bad because...
you can play Checkers or Slapjack with
your grandkids and let them win.

Gettin' old ain't so bad because...
you can rescue an adult cat or dog and
grow old together.

Gettin' old ain't so bad because...
you can share your wisdom by assisting
in a classroom.

Gettin' old ain't so bad because...
you don't have to worry...unless you want to.

Gettin' old ain't so bad because...
you can ride a bike or skateboard into your second childhood.

Gettin' old ain't so bad because...
you can go to the top of a roller coaster and scream like a kid!

Gettin' old ain't so bad because...
you can treat yourself to a manicure,
pedicure, facial, or massage. You
deserve it.

Gettin' old ain't so bad because...
you know you're beautiful on the inside,
where it counts.

Gettin' old ain't so bad because...
you can go back to school if you want,
and oftentimes classes are held at a
neighborhood senior center.

Gettin' old ain't so bad because...
if you want a bouquet of fresh flowers,
you can buy it for yourself.

Gettin' old ain't so bad because...
you can cook for two or one—or none.

Gettin' old ain't so bad because...
you finally have time to read the Bible
from Genesis to Revelation.

Gettin' old ain't so bad because...
you can take charge of the TV remote.

Gettin' old ain't so bad because...
you can turn down your hearing aids
when the noise is too loud.

Gettin' old ain't so bad because...
you can finally read the pile of
magazines on your nightstand.

Gettin' old ain't so bad because...
you can laugh at yourself and enjoy it.

Gettin' old ain't so bad because...
you can make new memories with
those you love.

Gettin' old ain't so bad because...
you can talk about "the good old days"
to the younger generation.

Gettin' old ain't so bad because...
you can finally let other people *be*.

Gettin' old ain't so bad because...
you can allow yourself to age gracefully
and gratefully.

Gettin' old ain't so bad because...
you can take long or short prayer walks with your honey.

Gettin' old ain't so bad because...
you can have a "granddog" without all the responsibilities of being an owner.

Gettin' old ain't so bad because...
you can entertain retired friends any time and for any reason.

Gettin' old ain't so bad because...
you can let go of people, places, and
things that wear you out.

Gettin' old ain't so bad because...
you can tell your family as often as you
want that you love them.

Gettin' old ain't so bad because...
you can make new "old" friends *and*
keep the old, old friends too.

Gettin' old ain't so bad because...
you can laugh at things you used to
worry about.

Gettin' old ain't so bad because...
you see that God's grace *is* new every
morning.

Gettin' old ain't so bad because...
you can listen to classical music morning, noon, and night if you want to.

Gettin' old ain't so bad because...
you can take a long motor trip alone or with another—your choice.

Gettin' old ain't so bad because...
you can mentor someone younger than you—and he or she might listen.

Gettin' old ain't so bad because...
you can plant tulip bulbs in the fall and enjoy a bouquet in the spring.

Gettin' old ain't so bad because...
you can show your grandkids how "hip" you are by texting them on your cell phone.

Gettin' old ain't so bad because...
you can train for a marathon if you
want to. No one can stop you!

Gettin' old ain't so bad because...
you have time to start a journal of
memories for each grandchild.

Gettin' old ain't so bad because...
if you lack wisdom, God promises to
give it to you—if you ask (James 1:5).

Gettin' old ain't so bad because...
you can enjoy window shopping and
not spend a penny.

Gettin' old ain't so bad because...
the sunsets and sunrises seem more
beautiful than ever.

Gettin' old ain't so bad because...
accepting yourself as you are is one of
the great benefits of aging.

Gettin' old ain't so bad because...
watching favorite old-time movies
brings back wonderful memories.

Gettin' old ain't so bad because...
at last, comfortable walking shoes are
more important than fashion footwear.

Gettin' old ain't so bad because...
sometimes it's nice to linger over the
dinner table before doing the dishes.

Gettin' old ain't so bad because...
it's fun to serve breakfast on your good
china without any questions.

Gettin' old ain't so bad because...
you can become a vegetarian now that
the kids are grown up.

Gettin' old ain't so bad because...
you can enjoy listening to the golden
oldies without criticism.

Gettin' old ain't so bad because...
you can splurge on season tickets to the
symphony or opera.

Gettin' old ain't so bad because...
you can try out for a community
theater production—even if it's only to
be a doorknob in the third act.

Gettin' old ain't so bad because...
you can pay for grandkids to attend
summer camp.

Gettin' old ain't so bad because...
now you have time to work on a photo
album of your childhood.

Gettin' old ain't so bad because...
you can rely more on prayer and less on
other people's opinions.

Gettin' old ain't so bad because...
there's still time to learn something new
and put it to use.

Gettin' old ain't so bad because...
it's easier now to forgive and forget.

Gettin' old ain't so bad because...
life is good and you're still able to share
it with others.

Gettin' old ain't so bad because...
it's time to listen to and love yourself
despite past behavior.

Gettin' old ain't so bad because...
you can keep on going—even if it takes
a cane or a walker.

Gettin' old ain't so bad because...
you don't have to associate with people
who pull you down.

Gettin' old ain't so bad because...
each day is new under the sun.

Gettin' old ain't so bad because...
you can now make the most of the time
you have.

Gettin' old ain't so bad because...
you can see that even small steps lead to
a desired goal.

Gettin' old ain't so bad because...
your wrinkles and white hair are a
testimony to your long life.

Gettin' old ain't so bad because...
it's better than the alternative.

Gettin' old ain't so bad because...
you can choose to wake up each
morning glad to be alive.

Gettin' old ain't so bad because...
you have a lot of support when you
need it—a cane, a banister, a helping
hand.

Gettin' old ain't so bad because...
you can enjoy lunch at a restaurant, a
matinee movie, and still be in bed by
eight.

Gettin' old ain't so bad because...
  you know when to speak your mind
  and when to hold your tongue.

Gettin' old ain't so bad because...
  you now eat your veggies on your own
  without being prompted.

Gettin' old ain't so bad because...
  you and your mate can each enjoy a
  favorite pastime and then talk about it.

Gettin' old ain't so bad because...
you can give up past resentments and
sleep soundly at night.

Gettin' old ain't so bad because...
the definition of success changes from
accomplishing goals to enjoying people.

Gettin' old ain't so bad because...
at last you can feel comfortable in your
own skin.

Gettin' old ain't so bad because...
you've learned to complain less and
appreciate more.

Gettin' old ain't so bad because...
you know where you've been and where
you want to go.

Gettin' old ain't so bad because...
you've given your kids roots and wings
and now you can release them to the Lord.

Gettin' old ain't so bad because...
you no longer have to pretend to be
nice. You can *be* genuinely nice to all.

Gettin' old ain't so bad because...
you can decide your own bedtime.

Gettin' old ain't so bad because...
you know how to entertain yourself
when others are busy.

Gettin' old ain't so bad because...
you have time to make a giant puzzle
on the floor with your grandchild.

Gettin' old ain't so bad because...
you have the opportunity to focus on
your talents instead of your limitations.

Gettin' old ain't so bad because...
younger people will want to be like you
when they grow up.

Gettin' old ain't so bad because...
you realize it takes so little to be above
average—if you put your mind to it.

Gettin' old ain't so bad because...
after a life well-lived, you are a truly
beautiful person.

Gettin' old ain't so bad because...
it's the ticket to a new kind of freedom
that is full of positive choices.

Gettin' old ain't so bad because...
you can say no without having to
explain.

Gettin' old ain't so bad because...
you can spoil the grandkids and get
away with it.

Gettin' old ain't so bad because...
you can blame your silly mistakes on
those pesky "senior moments."

Gettin' old ain't so bad because...
you can enhance your relationship
by taking turns. You go dancing on
Wednesday nights and your mate goes
on Fridays.

Gettin' old ain't so bad because...
when you don't have a choice, you can relax and let it go.

Gettin' old ain't so bad because...
the things that matter most don't cost a dime.

Gettin' old ain't so bad because...
a good life is a matter of attitude—not age.

Gettin' old ain't so bad because...
you've learned when to move forward,
when to stay put, and when to back off.

Gettin' old ain't so bad because...
you no longer have to hint about what
you want. You can say it outright.

Gettin' old ain't so bad because...
you can joke about your mistakes since
you have plenty of company.

Gettin' old ain't so bad because...
as long as you're still in the game, it doesn't matter who wins!

Gettin' old ain't so bad because...
you can agree or disagree and still be friends.

Gettin' old ain't so bad because...
dinner can be as simple as pancakes and syrup and who cares?

Gettin' old ain't so bad because...
your presence in people's lives is more important than your presents.

Gettin' old ain't so bad because...
expectations give way to expectancy.

Gettin' old ain't so bad because...
God is in charge so you don't have to be.

Gettin' old ain't so bad because...
you finally know when to back off and
when to move in.

Gettin' old ain't so bad because...
it's no longer "my way or the highway"
in marriage. It's *our* way all the way.

Gettin' old ain't so bad because...
being apart for a day from friend or spouse makes coming together that much sweeter.

Gettin' old ain't so bad because...
you don't have to make your bed unless you want to.

Gettin' old ain't so bad because...
you realize that empathy is much better than apathy.

Gettin' old ain't so bad because...
every day is a celebration of life.

Gettin' old ain't so bad because...
you're able to see God's light at the end
of every tunnel.

Gettin' old ain't so bad because...
you know you can't change others so
you stop trying.

Gettin' old ain't so bad because...
you realize that only God has the
answers you need.

Gettin' old ain't so bad because...
you find joy in seizing the moment—
and squeezing it!

Gettin' old ain't so bad because...
the best is yet to come—so keep going
till you get it.

Gettin' old ain't so bad because...
you can wear socks and sneakers nearly
anywhere at any time.

Gettin' old ain't so bad because...
you can eat the heart of a watermelon
and toss the rest without feeling guilty.

Gettin' old ain't so bad because...
you can eat a baked potato for breakfast
and cereal for dinner if you want to.

Gettin' old ain't so bad because...
you have more time behind you than
in front of you—so enjoy what's left to
the hilt.

Gettin' old ain't so bad because...
you can appreciate more than ever
the sights, sounds, smells, tastes, and
textures of a life well lived.

Gettin' old ain't so bad because...
you get to see yourself in your adult children and your adult children in yourself.

Gettin' old ain't so bad because...
you can talk to strangers in elevators without feeling self-conscious.

Gettin' old ain't so bad because...
younger people look up to you. How nice!

Gettin' old ain't so bad because...
you can give your living space a "good
enough" cleaning and be satisfied.

Gettin' old ain't so bad because...
you have the option of talking (or not)
when you feel like it.

Gettin' old ain't so bad because...
you can eat dessert first.

Gettin' old ain't so bad because...
you realize your viewpoint matters as
much as the next person's.

Gettin' old ain't so bad because...
you can learn from your grown
children and be proud of it.

Gettin' old ain't so bad because...
when life feels difficult you can
link arms and hearts without being
embarrassed.

Gettin' old ain't so bad because...
you can try new things like putting
salt on watermelon or peanut butter on
banana slices. Yum!

Gettin' old ain't so bad because...
playing jacks or jump rope with your
grandkids brings out the child in you.

Gettin' old ain't so bad because...
experience becomes more important
than accomplishments.

Gettin' old ain't so bad because...
it's never too late to learn how to
navigate Facebook and Twitter.

Gettin' old ain't so bad because...
everyone looks "older" at your class reunions.

Gettin' old ain't so bad because...
God's Word is a lamp to your feet and a light to your path (Psalm 119:105).

Gettin' old ain't so bad because...
your fears are fewer—if you make it so.

Gettin' old ain't so bad because...
each new day is filled with sweet
surprises.

Gettin' old ain't so bad because...
if you feel shaky, there is always
someone or something to lean on.

Gettin' old ain't so bad because...
when you bowl a strike or sink a putt
everyone pays attention.

Gettin' old ain't so bad because...
you can finally make your own decisions.

Gettin' old ain't so bad because...
you can get a discount on car insurance
if you take a mature driver's course.

Gettin' old ain't so bad because...
there is nothing you can't do—when
God leads.

Gettin' old ain't so bad because...
people notice and admire your stamina
and resilience.

Gettin' old ain't so bad because...
you can voice your opinion on the op/
ed page of the daily newspaper.

Gettin' old ain't so bad because...
you can go to the movies any hour and
pay a discounted price.

Gettin' old ain't so bad because...
you can soothe a crying baby with a
gentle lullaby.

Gettin' old ain't so bad because...
you can start a new career if you want to.

Gettin' old ain't so bad because...
you have more time for close friends.

Gettin' old ain't so bad because...
you can get rid of stuff you don't want
on eBay and make money doing so.

Gettin' old ain't so bad because...
you can live your goals instead of
dreaming about them.

Gettin' old ain't so bad because...
you can be impulsive if you feel like it.

Gettin' old ain't so bad because...
you're willing to say "I forgive you" and
mean it.

Gettin' old ain't so bad because...
each day you can discover what new
thing God has for you.

Gettin' old ain't so bad because...
if you lose your teeth you can buy new
ones.

Gettin' old ain't so bad because...
if you don't like what you're hearing
you can turn off your hearing aids.

Gettin' old ain't so bad because...
you can ignore bad memories and focus
on the good ones.

Gettin' old ain't so bad because...
you can repair broken relationships
before it's too late.

Gettin' old ain't so bad because...
it's time to replace negative thinking
with positive thoughts.

Gettin' old ain't so bad because...
you don't have to act older just because
you are.

Gettin' old ain't so bad because...
you'll never be bored if you commit to
lifelong learning.

Gettin' old ain't so bad because...
you get to be a blessing to everyone
around you.

Gettin' old ain't so bad because...
you can eliminate procrastination by
doing one thing each day that needs
doing.

Gettin' old ain't so bad because...
you can sort out what is useful
knowledge and what wastes your time.

Gettin' old ain't so bad because...
you can choose to be thoughtful and
gracious instead of difficult and fault-
finding.

Gettin' old ain't so bad because...
 you can rest in the promises of God.

Gettin' old ain't so bad because...
 you can watch the cartoon channel and
 admit it.

Gettin' old ain't so bad because...
 you have more opportunities to smile
 than to weep.

Gettin' old ain't so bad because...
you realize there is a season—and a reason—for everything under the sun.

Gettin' old ain't so bad because...
you can enjoy fishing even if you don't catch anything.

Gettin' old ain't so bad because...
you can do something special for yourself and not feel guilty.

Gettin' old ain't so bad because...
you can do more things you want to do
and less of those you don't want to do.

Gettin' old ain't so bad because...
you can make someone's day with a
warm smile or hearty handshake.

Gettin' old ain't so bad because...
you can spend time alone and enjoy it.

Gettin' old ain't so bad because...
you can share your point of view with others without imposing it on them.

Gettin' old ain't so bad because...
you can see more beauty in diversity.

Gettin' old ain't so bad because...
you can trust yourself to make wise choices.

Gettin' old ain't so bad because...
you have time to enjoy a play day with a grandchild.

Gettin' old ain't so bad because...
you don't have to make school lunches for your kids anymore.

Gettin' old ain't so bad because...
loving others becomes a top priority.

Gettin' old ain't so bad because...
you know that God loves you and that's
what really matters.

Gettin' old ain't so bad because...
you can sit back and observe without
judgment.

Gettin' old ain't so bad because...
you're willing and able to find the good
in people as never before.

Gettin' old ain't so bad because...
it's never too late to say "I'm sorry."

Gettin' old ain't so bad because...
you know smiling is more healing than frowning.

Gettin' old ain't so bad because...
you're more likely now to pay attention to where you put your dentures or parked your car.

Gettin' old ain't so bad because...
you discover there's no day as lovely as
this one.

Gettin' old ain't so bad because...
you can finally eat to live instead of
living to eat.

Gettin' old ain't so bad because...
you know the truth when you hear it.

Gettin' old ain't so bad because...
you can smooth out a wretched day
with a chocolate-filled croissant.

Gettin' old ain't so bad because...
you can enjoy a movie a second time
because you probably don't remember
the plot anyway.

Gettin' old ain't so bad because...
a "second childhood" gives you a
chance to make up for what you missed
the first time around.

Gettin' old ain't so bad because...
you know how to face and get over
stressful experiences.

Gettin' old ain't so bad because...
you have more time to review old photos or reread your journals and love letters.

Gettin' old ain't so bad because...
you're not too proud to ask for advice when you need it.

Gettin' old ain't so bad because...
you realize the value of clear family communication.

Gettin' old ain't so bad because...
you know how to avoid the triggers that
harm loving relationships.

Gettin' old ain't so bad because...
a good book and a cup of tea can turn an
ordinary day into an extraordinary one.

Gettin' old ain't so bad because...
strong, long-term friendships are better
than gold.

Gettin' old ain't so bad because...
every new day is a blessing regardless of
the circumstances.

Gettin' old ain't so bad because...
the wisdom you've acquired can be put
to good use.

Gettin' old ain't so bad because...
God's Word guides you in all areas of life.

Gettin' old ain't so bad because...
you know when you affirm others, they
will affirm you.

Gettin' old ain't so bad because...
you have countless opportunities to
let go of anger and choose compassion
instead.

Gettin' old ain't so bad because...
you see the value of humor in almost
every situation.

Gettin' old ain't so bad because...
you see that everyone needs a pat on the
back—and you are available to give it!

Gettin' old ain't so bad because...
years of life experience have taught you
to give your burdens to God.

Gettin' old ain't so bad because...
you know how to apply wisdom and
discernment to every relationship.

Gettin' old ain't so bad because...
whatever comes your way you know
you can handle it by the grace of God.

Gettin' old ain't so bad because...
you have many positive memories to help you through life's temporary storms.

Gettin' old ain't so bad because...
after years of living life your way, you're now rooted in God's wisdom.

Gettin' old ain't so bad because...
you're more willing to live one day at a time.

Gettin' old ain't so bad because...
when push comes to shove, you know
to step aside so no one gets hurt.

Gettin' old ain't so bad because...
you know the importance of doing
what needs to be done—even if you
don't feel like it.

Gettin' old ain't so bad because...
by now you know that being kind is
more important than being right.

Gettin' old ain't so bad because...
you appreciate your body more so you
set aside time to take care of it.

Gettin' old ain't so bad because...
you know the value of an encouraging
word and you give it freely.

Gettin' old ain't so bad because...
you can appreciate how a walk in
nature calms your spirit.

Gettin' old ain't so bad because...
you're more open to the good in life all
around you.

Gettin' old ain't so bad because...
you realize how blessed you've been.

Gettin' old ain't so bad because...
you know that each breath you take is a gift from God.

Gettin' old ain't so bad because...
the past is over and the future is before you.

Gettin' old ain't so bad because...
you can be a grandparent to a child who doesn't have any.

Gettin' old ain't so bad because...
 you can give a compliment a day to
 keep the blues away.

Gettin' old ain't so bad because...
 you can count on God when the going
 gets tough.

Gettin' old ain't so bad because...
 you can bring out your playful self
 without being embarrassed.

Gettin' old ain't so bad because...
you realize the key to a good
relationship is listening more than
speaking.

Gettin' old ain't so bad because...
silly stuff that mattered when you were
younger has fallen away.

Gettin' old ain't so bad because...
you enjoy recounting the good old days
with dear friends.

Gettin' old ain't so bad because...
even though your body is slowing down,
your spirit is willing to keep going.

Gettin' old ain't so bad because...
the prayers of a caring friend will help
you get through a difficult day.

Gettin' old ain't so bad because...
you can go to two or three movies in
one day—if you want to.

Gettin' old ain't so bad because...
you can put on a favorite CD and
dance around the living room in your
house slippers.

Gettin' old ain't so bad because...
you have the freedom to do absolutely
nothing all day long if you want to.

Gettin' old ain't so bad because...
you can hike the mountains or walk the
beach with other seniors who go at your
pace.

Gettin' old ain't so bad because...
you can hop a bus and see the sights in
your hometown anytime.

Gettin' old ain't so bad because...
you can eat sweets whenever you please.

Gettin' old ain't so bad because...
you know the importance of making
every day a day of praise.

Gettin' old ain't so bad because...
"For this God is our God for ever and
ever; he will be our guide even to the
end" (Psalm 48:14).

Gettin' old ain't so bad because...
you can misplace your glasses or car
keys and know the Lord will lead you
to them.

Gettin' old ain't so bad because...
you've lived long enough to know God
is in charge and all is well.

Gettin' old ain't so bad because...
you finally realize that everyone is
entitled to his or her point of view.

Gettin' old ain't so bad because...
now you see that you don't know
everything and you never will. And
you're okay with that.

Gettin' old ain't so bad because...
you can love extravagantly and never run dry.

Gettin' old ain't so bad because...
you can laugh at yourself.

Gettin' old ain't so bad because...
you know everything will turn out for good in the long run.

Gettin' old ain't so bad because...
you know the importance of a good
night's sleep…so you enjoy it.

Gettin' old ain't so bad because...
you're positive God loves you with an
everlasting love—regardless of your
mistakes.

Gettin' old ain't so bad because...
you know that what matters is
transformation not information.

Gettin' old ain't so bad because...
you know that a sense of humor adds
zest to your life.

Gettin' old ain't so bad because...
you recognize you're one of God's
choice possessions.

Gettin' old ain't so bad because...
  you're aware that the most satisfying
  lifestyle is one of authenticity.

Gettin' old ain't so bad because...
  you can count on Jesus as the way, the
  truth, and the life.

Gettin' old ain't so bad because...
you can wear comfy clothes and not apologize for it.

Gettin' old ain't so bad because...
you can ask for a hug without being embarrassed.

Gettin' old ain't so bad because...
you can stay up all night reading, playing on the computer, or watching movies if you want to.

Gettin' old ain't so bad because...
you can share your opinions and not get upset if others don't agree.

Gettin' old ain't so bad because...
you can be spontaneous and playful for no reason.

Gettin' old ain't so bad because...
you can go out for a hamburger at midnight if you want to.

Gettin' old ain't so bad because...
you've learned that outward beauty is
only skin deep, but inward beauty lasts
a lifetime.

Gettin' old ain't so bad because...
you know where to look when you're in
sorrow—*up!*

Gettin' old ain't so bad because...
you enjoy the simple things, such as a
walk in the park.

Gettin' old ain't so bad because...
you know without a doubt that God
will remember your sins no more
(Jeremiah 31:34).

Gettin' old ain't so bad because...
you can find ways to help the hurting
and help yourself at the same time.

Gettin' old ain't so bad because...
you learn something positive from every
problem.

Gettin' old ain't so bad because...
you know kindness overcomes criticism.

Gettin' old ain't so bad because...
you bask in the glow of the warm
memories you've made with loved ones.

Gettin' old ain't so bad because...
 you know "the gift of God is eternal life
 in Christ Jesus" (Romans 6:23).

Gettin' old ain't so bad because...
 you have time to learn a new skill or
 take up a new hobby.

Gettin' old ain't so bad because...
 you can support others by offering
 understanding instead of advice.

Gettin' old ain't so bad because...
you know how to be polite in tight
situations.

Gettin' old ain't so bad because...
you know hope will keep you going
when you feel like giving up.

Gettin' old ain't so bad because...
you can take a trip using money you've saved for a rainy day.

Gettin' old ain't so bad because...
you can see the bright side of things more easily than the dark side.

Gettin' old ain't so bad because...
you can prepare a feast or a snack just for you.

Gettin' old ain't so bad because...
you know the value of saying "I love you" often.

Gettin' old ain't so bad because...
you have a better understanding of how the world works.

Gettin' old ain't so bad because...
you can skip the dishes and say yes to a last-minute invitation.

Gettin' old ain't so bad because...
you can enjoy a quiet night alone
without feeling lonely.

Gettin' old ain't so bad because...
you know that little things, such as
holding hands and laughing together,
are essential.

Gettin' old ain't so bad because...
you know that a drive in the country
will improve your mood.

Gettin' old ain't so bad because...
you have time to serve others in small
ways.

Gettin' old ain't so bad because...
you know that a helping hand is one of
the best gifts of all.

Gettin' old ain't so bad because...
you realize how little cat naps can lift
your spirit.

Gettin' old ain't so bad because...
you know from experience that "a
cheerful heart is good medicine"
(Proverbs 17:22).

Gettin' old ain't so bad because...
you've learned the importance of
pumping iron as you age.

Gettin' old ain't so bad because...
you're able to listen between the lines.

Gettin' old ain't so bad because...
you can freely give credit where credit
is due.

Gettin' old ain't so bad because...
you know how to bounce back from
pain and loss.

Gettin' old ain't so bad because...
you know faith can triumph over fear.

Gettin' old ain't so bad because...
you can dance away your cares before
the Lord.

Gettin' old ain't so bad because...
you know how to have fun with or
without money.

Gettin' old ain't so bad because...
you've learned to be flexible about
almost everything.

Gettin' old ain't so bad because...
you can tell the truth in loving ways.

Gettin' old ain't so bad because...
you're willing to be your true self in all
situations.

Gettin' old ain't so bad because...
you know how to inspire young people
with your example.

Gettin' old ain't so bad because...
you can accept yourself for who you are
and be grateful.

Gettin' old ain't so bad because...
you know how to cherish and respect
those you love.

Gettin' old ain't so bad because...
you can control yourself when you feel
upset.

Gettin' old ain't so bad because...
you're able to bring peace to stressful situations.

Gettin' old ain't so bad because...
you let the Holy Spirit be your Comforter when you're afraid or sad.

Gettin' old ain't so bad because...
you know you can't change circum-stances—only how you react to them.

Gettin' old ain't so bad because...
you realize that prayer is the answer to most challenges.

Gettin' old ain't so bad because...
you know kind words never go out of style.

Gettin' old ain't so bad because...
you know a hug will go a long way to
resolve difficulties with your spouse or
friend.

Gettin' old ain't so bad because...
you're aware that each day brings its
own blessings.

Gettin' old ain't so bad because...
there is still time to dream big.

Gettin' old ain't so bad because...
there is *always* something to look
forward to.

Gettin' old ain't so bad because...
with God in charge, there is nothing to
fear.

Gettin' old ain't so bad because...
you have time to reflect on the ups and
downs of your life and learn from them.

Gettin' old ain't so bad because...
you know everyone loses when playing
the blame game.

Gettin' old ain't so bad because...
you always look for positive qualities in
others.

Gettin' old ain't so bad because...
you know that God's purpose is to give you life in all its fullness (John 10:10).

Gettin' old ain't so bad because...
you know that the more you accept people's differences, the more likely they'll accept yours.

Gettin' old ain't so bad because...
you can disagree with someone you love without being disagreeable.

Gettin' old ain't so bad because...
you know how to be content wherever
you are.

Gettin' old ain't so bad because...
you can cry when you're sad, knowing
God will dry your tears.

Gettin' old ain't so bad because...
you have so much to be grateful for...
and you say it.

Gettin' old ain't so bad because...
life is no longer about winning. It's about loving.

Gettin' old ain't so bad because...
you've learned the power of going the extra mile whenever possible.

Gettin' old ain't so bad because...
now you have time to write your memoir.

Gettin' old ain't so bad because...
you know the value of volunteering to help your community—and you have the time to do so.

Gettin' old ain't so bad because...
you know your words of support will help a friend or spouse "lose" his or her temper.

Gettin' old ain't so bad because...
when your mate misplaces his
whatchamacallit you can help by
sharing your thingamagig.

Gettin' old ain't so bad because...
you know that a word to the wise is
sufficient only if you apply it.

Gettin' old ain't so bad because...
you've learned it's better to put out the
fire of anger than to let it smolder.

Gettin' old ain't so bad because...
minute by minute you can choose to go
in a new direction.

Gettin' old ain't so bad because...
you can give up "shoulda" and "woulda."

Gettin' old ain't so bad because...
one day your life on earth will end
and you'll be forever happy in God's
presence.

Gettin' old ain't so bad because...
you know from experience that God
can and will meet all your needs.

Gettin' old ain't so bad because...
you've learned that a life worth living is a life filled with love.

Gettin' old ain't so bad because...
you know God sustains you (Isaiah 46:4).

Gettin' old ain't so bad because...
you can hold your tongue when you need to.

Karen O'Connor

*Opening hearts and connecting lives
through writing and speaking*

Karen has authored many magazine articles and books, including the bestselling *Bein' a Grandparent Ain't for Wimps*. She's won numerous awards, including the Paul A. Witty Award for short story writing (International Reading Assoc., 2005). A sought-after speaker, Karen enthusiastically and humorously inspires people to...

- experience and express more joy and gratitude
- embrace positive growth
- achieve greater intimacy with God, self, and others
- polish communication and leadership skills

For more information about Karen, her books, her speaking, or to share with her why you believe the golden years are great, contact:

Karen O'Connor Communications
10 Pajaro Vista Court
Watsonville, CA 95076
Phone: 831-768-7335

Email: Karen@KarenOconnor.com

Gettin' Old Ain't for Wimps

Bursting with wit and wisdom, these lighthearted, real-life stories, insightful Scriptures, and heartfelt prayers will make you chuckle and confess "That sounds just like me!" Popular speaker and author Karen O'Connor invites you to celebrate the joys and misadventures of getting older. Have you noticed that...

- when you can't find your glasses, they're usually on your head?
- the delightful honesty of youth sometimes bites?
- love still makes your heart skip a beat ... or two ... or three?

Are you ready to trade in your wimp status for a more courageous existence? *Gettin' Old Ain't for Wimps* hilariously affirms that life will always be filled with wonder, promise, and adventure!